THE COMP
IRISH TINWHISTLE
TUNEBOOK

by L.E. McCullough.

Oak Publications
New York/London/Paris/Sydney/Copenhagen/Madrid

Project editor: Peter Pickow
Chord notation: Don Meade

Order No. OK 65021
US International Standard Book Number: 0.8256.0341.2
UK International Standard Book Number: 0.7119.8984.2

Exclusive Distributors:
Music Sales Corporation
257 Park Avenue South, New York, NY 10010 USA
Music Sales Limited
8/9 Frith Street, London W1D 3JB England
Music Sales Pty. Limited
120 Rothschild Street, Rosebery, Sydney, NSW 2018, Australia

Printed in the United States of America by
Vicks Lithograph and Printing Corporation

DOUBLE JIGS

SINGLE JIGS

SLIP JIGS

REELS

SET DANCES

AIRS

MISCELLANEOUS

Introduction

Perhaps the most challenging thing to master when learning to play traditional Irish music is the ability to play "in sync" with other musicians. *The Complete Irish Tinwhistle Tunebook* gives you the chance to do exactly that. It is a collection of 125 tunes you're liable to hear at most traditional Irish music sessions. Once you have these tunes under your belt and in your fingers, you'll be able to sit down with a group of Irish musicians anywhere in the world and play with comfort and confidence.

In the Irish tradition, the session (or *seisiún,* as it's called in Irish Gaelic) is the chief means of exchanging tunes among players. Some would say that the session is the very heart of the tradition, since it keeps the repertoire fresh by mixing old favorites with new or lesser-known compositions. If you're a beginning musician, the session is the best place to hear new tunes and the best place to play tunes you've just learned.

Very few hermits play traditional Irish music. It is a music that has, for the last several centuries, been a highly social activity performed at a wide range of public and private venues. A session can occur anywhere at any moment—in a pub or restaurant, at a park or dance or concert, in airport and hotel lobbies, on any sidewalk in any city in the world. I once played in a session on a Greyhound bus to Galveston, Texas. Another time I encountered a red-hot session on the platform of a New York subway station. Then there was the session that broke out at 3 A.M. in the back lot of an all-night Dunkin' Donuts in Brattleboro, Vermont . . . you get the point.

The typical session isn't very formal, though every session follows a certain unspoken but quickly established etiquette of who starts a tune, how many times a tune is played before ending, when another tune is introduced, and so forth. A session quickly establishes its own pace and character, defined largely by the tunes played. It's like a conversation, an expanded dialogue among musicians that ebbs and flows in mood from laid-back and easygoing to intense and even frenzied. For an in-depth—and often irreverent and hilariously incisive—look at the social dynamics and curious rituals of sessions, check this book by Seattle musician Barry Foy: *Field Guide to the Irish Music Session* (Roberts Rinehart, 1999).

The best thing about an Irish music session is that anyone can participate. The price of admission? Knowing a few tunes the other musicians can play along with you. If you learn the tunes in this book and in *The Complete Irish Tinwhistle Tutor,* you'll have almost 200 tunes as a core repertoire, and that's all it takes to get started.

The Complete Irish Tinwhistle Tunebook CD is designed for easy learning. A tune is played slowly first and with minimal ornamentation. The second time through, the tune goes a bit faster and with more ornaments and even some common variations, so you can experience some of the exciting unpredictability of a real session! Most musicians will tell you that the best way to learn Irish traditional music is by ear, but having a standard reference point is vital, and that's what the notated versions in the book provide.

The Complete Irish Tinwhistle Tunebook also contains chord notation in the book and easy-to-follow chord progressions by guitarist Don Meade and pianist Brendan Dolan on the CD. While the harmonic structure of Irish music is not overly complex, it does contain numerous subtleties, and a skilled backup player will use many variant progressions when playing along even with simple tunes. In the chord notations herein, a chord in parentheses (**D**) indicates an optional chord at that point in the tune. But these aren't the only "correct" chords, so keep your eyes and ears open to what other accompanists are doing.

In traditional Irish music the notation of the melody and rhythm is always "approximate." There simply isn't room on the staff for all of what's happening on the instrument. In this book, the ornamentation details have been kept very simple, using not much more than short and long rolls and a few triplets. On the next page are examples of short and long rolls on G.

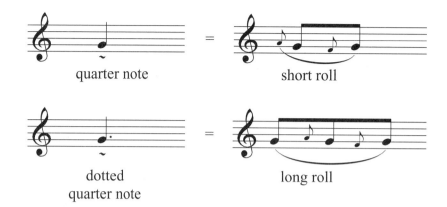

quarter note   short roll

dotted
quarter note   long roll

Rolls can be executed on any note of the scale; the exact grace notes within each roll will depend upon what instrument you're playing. When you see a quarter note, you can use a short roll to replace it; when you see a dotted quarter note, you can use a long roll.

You may already know how to "translate" the unornamented melodic line into the traditional performing style that includes rolls, graces, triplets, and slurs. If not, consult *The Complete Irish Tinwhistle Tutor* book and CD for a thorough explanation of basic ornamental techniques in Irish music.

You don't need to master every ornament when first learning a tune. Learn the basic skeleton of the melody, but remain flexible enough to incorporate variations when you hear them. You'll quickly discover there are many versions of an Irish tune, some very similar, some radically different; Irish music is one of the most fluid and elastic musical idioms on the planet. As long as you have a solid grip on at least one version, you'll fit in with the other players and get into the flow of the session.

And the session is where the music truly lives—in the hearts and souls of reelmakers and jigcrafters everywhere.

L. E. McCullough
Teach Áthas
3 October 2001

Accompanying Irish Traditional Dance Tunes

The eighteenth- and nineteenth-century musicians whose reels, jigs, and hornpipes still dominate the Irish traditional repertoire generally played without benefit of accompaniment. Uilleann pipers with their drones and regulators could provide their own backing, but fiddlers, fluters, and tinwhistle players contented themselves with the bare melodic line.

Like other popular recordings of the day, the 78-rpm discs of Irish music made during the ethnic recording boom of the 1920s and '30s usually included piano accompaniment. Some of these pianists had a good ear for Irish music, but others succeeded only in ruining otherwise worthy recordings.

Guitar accompaniment began to infiltrate the traditional music scene in the 1930s. The guitar's lighter sound and lower volume made it a better match for a solo player, and the instrument had a great appeal to the guitar-oriented generation that launched the folk revival of the 1960s. The bouzouki, introduced to Irish music in the mid 1960s, was thought by many to be even better suited to the drones and modal harmonies of Irish traditional music. Irish guitarists in recent years, in fact, have often sought to capture a bouzouki-like sound with nonstandard tunings such as DADGAD.

The chords used in this book should be viewed as suggestions rather than hard-and-fast prescriptions. In many cases, a variety of possible harmonic choices exist. A single drone chord can often be substituted for a series of rapid changes. You can often replace major chords with their relative minors—E Minor for G, B Minor for D, A Minor for C, *etc.* You may also wish to experiment with modal harmonies by playing chords with the root and fifth alone in place of full major or minor triads—G and D notes for a G or G Minor chord, D and A notes for a D or D Minor chord, A and E notes for an A or A Minor chord, *etc.* Adventurous players may wish to try their hand at more complex jazz chords. In seeking sophistication, however, one should never forget that Irish dance tunes and airs can still sound just fine even when totally unaccompanied!

DON MEADE

Compact Disc: 1
Practice Track: 1
Performance Track: 2

The Battering Ram

Heard at a lively session during a ceili *at the West Side Irish-American Club, Cleveland, Ohio (May 1973)—*
featuring Tom Byrne on flute, Al ÓLaoire on accordion, and Tom McCafferty on fiddle.

Compact Disc: 1
Practice Track: 3
Performance Track: 4

Bímíd ag Ól

Heard during a session at the Four Seasons Pub in Dublin (April 1972) with fiddlers John Kelly, Sr., and Joe Ryan.

Compact Disc: I
Practice Track: 5
Performance Track: 6

Boys of the Town

From a session at fiddler Paddy Cronin's home, West Roxbury, Massachusetts (June 1973).

Cook in the Kitchen

From uilleann piper Joe McKenna, Thomas Street Pipers' Club, Dublin (April 1972).

Compact Disc: 1
Practice Track: 9
Performance Track: 10

DRUMSHAMBO JIG

Heard on Phyllis Brzowzsksa's front porch, Yellow Springs, Ohio (June 1978), from the group Devilish Merry—
Burr Beard (hammered dulcimer), Larry Edelman (mandolin), Jan Hamilton (fiddle), and Sue Powers (five-string banjo).

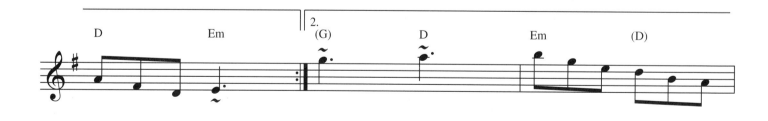

Compact Disc: 1
Practice Track: 11
Performance Track: 12

DUSTY WINDOWSILL

*A composition by Chicago tinwhistler Johnny Harling first heard from fiddler Liz Carroll
at the Chicago Feis, Chicago, Illinois (June 1980).*

Compact Disc: 1
Practice Track: 13
Performance Track: 14

East at Glendart

From fiddler Patrick Ourceau, uilleann piper Jerry O'Sullivan, and tenor banjoist Don Meade
at Kate Kearney's, New York City (February 1997).

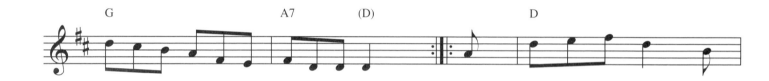

Compact Disc: 1
Practice Track: 15
Performance Track: 16

THE FROST IS ALL OVER

From flute player/uilleann piper Kevin Henry at Flanagan's Pub, Chicago (May 1978).

Compact Disc: 1
Practice Track: 17
Performance Track: 18

GEESE IN THE BOG

From uilleann piper Brian Gallagher at the Wren's Nest, Chapelizod, Ireland (March 1972).

| Compact Disc: 1 |
| Practice Track: 19 |
| Performance Track: 20 |

GILLIAN'S APPLES

From fiddlers Erin Shrader and Eric Miller at a house ceili, Bloomington, Indiana (September 1996).

Compact Disc: 1
Practice Track: 21
Performance Track: 22

Hare in the Corn

Heard in June 1978 at the Blarney Stone, Pittsburgh, Pennsylvania, featuring the members of Clanjamfrey—
uilleann piper Bruce Foley, mandolinist Pete Farley, concertina player Dave Paton, and bouzouki player Truck Croteau.

Compact Disc: 1
Practice Track: 23
Performance Track: 24

Killina Jig

From tinwhistler Peter Suk at the Riley School of Irish Music, Cincinnati, Ohio (February 1999);
also known as "The Hag at the Kiln."

Compact Disc: 1
Practice Track: 25
Performance Track: 26

Langstrom's Pony

From uilleann piper Bill Ochs at the Mushroom Bar, Greenwich Village (June 1973).

Compact Disc: 1
Practice Track: 27
Performance Track: 28

LARK ON THE STRAND

From uilleann piper Dennis Igoe, flutist Noel Rice, and fiddler Phillipe Varlet
during the Comhaltas Ceoltoiri Eireann *national convention, Tarrytown, New York (April 1995).*

Compact Disc: 1
Practice Track: 29
Performance Track: 30

Maid at the Well

From a session at the Bard's, Philadelphia (February 1996), with Roy Rogers (uilleann pipes), Hollis Payton (fiddle), Jack Crowley (tenor banjo), Bob Michel (flute), Bil McKenty (tinwhistle), and Ed Clark (bodhrán).

Maid on the Green

From flutist Richard Hughes at an annual Scrimshaw Party hosted by folk impresario Stuart Cohen, Pittsburgh (February 1975).

Compact Disc: I
Practice Track: 33
Performance Track: 34

The Monaghan Jig

From fiddler Martin Wynne at the family home of fiddler Brian Conway, Brooklyn, New York (December 1977).

Compact Disc: I
Practice Track: 35
Performance Track: 36

The Nefarious Jig

A composition of tenor banjoist John "Johnny Banjo" Woodard heard in March 1991 at a session hosted by Matt O'Neill
at the Fluttering Duck Pub in Greencastle, Indiana, and featuring the Black Walnut Boys.

Old Man Dillon

Heard April 1974 from flutist David Molk and fiddler Tom Sparks playing in People's Park, Bloomington, Indiana.

Compact Disc: I
Practice Track: 39
Performance Track: 40

OLD TIPPERARY

From uilleann piper Tim Britton street-busking in Center City, Philadelphia (July 1977).

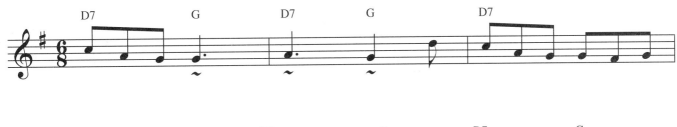

Compact Disc: I
Practice Track: 41
Performance Track: 42

Paddy Clancy's Jig

Heard May 1994 at one of the monthly square dances in Woodstock, New York,
hosted by fiddler Jay Ungar and guitarist Molly Mason.

PULL THE KNIFE AND STICK IT AGAIN

From Chris Davala (concertina) and Lisa Vandergrift (flute) at a session on their farm in East Clare (August 1976).

Compact Disc: I
Practice Track: 45
Performance Track: 46

THE RAMBLES OF KITTY

From fiddler Pat Keogh at the Wallace Wedding, Ashokan, New York (September 2000).

Compact Disc: 1
Practice Track: 47
Performance Track: 48

THE ROOKERY

From tinwhistler Albert Neary and fiddlers Phil Durkin and Pat Burke at the Midwest Fleadh Ceoil, *Chicago (May 1974); often called "Whelan's Jig."*

Compact Disc: 1
Practice Track: 49
Performance Track: 50

Rose in the Heather

From Rick Gagne (tenor banjo), Jeremy Goode (tinwhistle), and Mark Dawson (guitar) at a house session,
Indianapolis, Indiana (May 1991).

Scotsman over the Border

Heard at a roof-raising pub session at the Fleadh Ceoil na hÉireann, *Buncrana, Donegal (August 1975),*
featuring no less than eight bodhrán players and one stalwart unknown accordionist from Portugal.

Compact Disc: I
Practice Track: 53
Performance Track: 54

Thrush in the Straw

From Grey Larsen (flute) and Malcolm Dalglish (hammered dulcimer) at a ceili *in Cincinnati (October 1981); also known as "Mist in the Meadow."*

Compact Disc: 1
Practice Track: 55
Performance Track: 56

Tobin's Favorite

From flutist Cathal McConnell during a session following a Boys of the Lough concert at Calliope House, Pittsburgh (April 1980).

Compact Disc: 1
Practice Track: 57
Performance Track: 58

Tom Billy's Jig

From fiddler Rebecca Miller at the opening of the new Anyone Can Whistle music store, Kingston, New York (August 1994).

TRIP TO ATHLONE

*Also called "The Newport Lass," I heard this July 1976 at the Festival of American Folklife in Washington, D.C.,
during a session featuring the Irish group De Danaan; the entire festival week was a tribute to Irish and American Irish music
sponsored by the Smithsonian Institute.*

Compact Disc: 1
Practice Track: 61
Performance Track: 62

Lisheen Slide No. 1

From fiddlers James and John Kelly, Jr., during a session at the Kelly home, Dublin (May 1972).

Compact Disc: 1
Practice Track: 63
Performance Track: 64

Lisheen Slide No. 2

From fiddlers James and John Kelly, Jr., during a session at the Kelly home, Dublin (May 1972).

O'Keefe's Slide

From a ceili *featuring fiddlers Una McGlew, Mary McDonagh, and Maida Sugrue and concertina/accordion player Terry Teahan, Highland Hall, Chicago (April 1977).*

THE PAPER PLATE

This came from a house session on Chicago's Northside with Terry Teahan (April 1976).

Compact Disc: 1
Practice Track: 69
Performance Track: 70

Barney Brallaghan

*From a session featuring tinwhistle player Geraldine Murray and guitarist Nancy Conescu,
Biddy McGraw's, Portland, Oregon (March 1999).*

Compact Disc: 1
Practice Track: 71
Performance Track: 72

DEVER THE DANCER

From a ceili at Mullaney's Harp and Fiddle, Pittsburgh, featuring tinwhistle player Carla Dundes, fiddlers Richard Moore and Peter Shovlin, and bodhránist Les Getschell (October 2000).

Compact Disc: 1
Practice Track: 73
Performance Track: 74

Hardiman the Fiddler

From a house session in Cumberland, Indiana (October 1990), featuring Don Latham (five-string banjo),
Alberta Latham (tinwhistle), Steve Kobe (mandolin), and Jean Stewart (guitar).

D.C.

Compact Disc: I
Practice Track: 75
Performance Track: 76

The Swaggering Jig

*From uilleann piper Pat Sky, flutist Mark Roberts, and bouzouki player Billy Crozier (the Potstill Band)
at the Bottom Line, New York City (December 1977).*

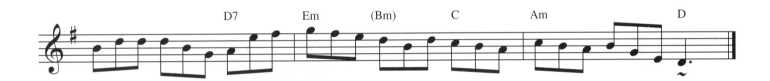

THE ABBEY REEL

Compact Disc: 2
Practice Track: 1
Performance Track: 2

From fiddler Liz Carroll during a session at the Atlantic Restaurant, Chicago (July 1977).

D.C.

THE ASH PLANT

From accordionists Jimmy Thornton and Pat Clooney at a St. Patrick's Night Party,
13th Ward Democratic Club, Chicago (March 1976).

Compact Disc: 2
Practice Track: 5
Performance Track: 6

Boil the Breakfast Early

From a session at the Starry Plough, Berkeley, California (August 1999), following the wedding of J.D. and Mary Nelson.

Boy in the Gap

From a session at the Seattle Tionol *(February 1996) featuring fiddlers Dale Russ and Paul Michel,*
uilleann piper Todd Denman, and flutist Barry Foy.

Compact Disc: 2
Practice Track: 9
Performance Track: 10

THE BROKEN PLEDGE

From a session featuring uilleann piper/fiddler Fiona Doherty, accordionist Patty Furlong, and pianist Brendan Dolan at Ryan's Pub, New York City (January 1996).

CALLAGHAN'S REEL

From a session in a Dublin flat (August 1976) with fiddler Armin Barnett and uilleann pipers Bill Ochs and Tim Britton.

D.C.

Compact Disc: 2
Practice Track: 13
Performance Track: 14

CAPTAIN KELLY

From accordionist Paddy O'Brien during a session at fiddler Barb Zavon's house, Cincinnati, Ohio (October 1981).

D.C.

Compact Disc: 2
Practice Track: 15
Performance Track: 16

CHRISTMAS EVE

From flutists Jack Coen and Mike Rafferty backed by guitarist Jimmy Coen at the Leeds Irish Festival, Leeds, New York (July 1994); this popular reel is a composition of Galway fiddler Tommy Coen.

Connemara Stocking

From flutist Michael Gallagher, in a session at his home, Pittsburgh (November 1974).

Compact Disc: 2
Practice Track: 17
Performance Track: 18

THE COPPERPLATE NO. 1

A popular reel often heard during sessions following the Irish Hour *radio show
at Chicago's Hibernian Hall hosted by Martin Fahey, Sr. (March 1974).*

Compact Disc: 2
Practice Track: 21
Performance Track: 22

THE COPPERPLATE No. 2

From a session in July 1977 at the Francis O'Neill Music Club, Chicago, featuring flute players Noel Rice and Pat McPartland and accordionists Tom O'Malley and John Murray with backing by Mary McDonagh on piano.

Compact Disc: 2
Practice Track: 23
Performance Track: 24

CRAIG'S PIPES

From a session at the Fort Wayne Irish Festival, Fort Wayne, Indiana (August 1999), with Kim Hoffman (guitar),
T.H. Gillespie (bass), Leslie Krom-Selden (fiddle), and Bernie (fiddle) and Tom (tinwhistle) Lohmuller.

Dick Gossip's Reel

Heard at a session by unknown players during the Freehold Feis, Freehold Raceway, New Jersey (June 1973).

The Doon Reel

From Pat (uilleann pipes) and Cathy (fiddle) Sky at a ceili in Chapel Hill, North Carolina (May 1993);
also known as "The Mountain Top."

Compact Disc: 2
Practice Track: 29
Performance Track: 30

Duke of Leinster

Learned from fiddler Michael Kelly, Spread Eagle Bar, London (April 1972).

Compact Disc: 2
Practice Track: 31
Performance Track: 32

THE FIVE-MILE CHASE

Heard from mandolinist Mark Bickford and guitarist Charlie Mills at Waterloo Ice House, Austin, Texas (February 1985).

Compact Disc: 2
Practice Track: 33
Performance Track: 34

Fred Finn's Reel

From a session at the Martin Mulvihill home featuring fiddlers Martin and Brendan Mulvihill, flutist Gus Collins,
and accordionist John O'Leary, The Bronx, New York (June 1973), with the title commemorating Sligo fiddler Fred Finn.

Compact Disc: **2**
Practice Track: 35
Performance Track: 36

GLEN ALLEN

*Heard in a session featuring guitarists Ed Miller, Rich Brotherton, and Pipo Hernandez
at Colorado Street Cafe, Austin, Texas (July 1988); also known as "The Kilmaley Reel."*

Compact Disc: 2
Practice Track: 37
Performance Track: 38

Green Mountain

From a session at the house of five-string banjoist Kevin Donnelly, Indianapolis (October 1990).

Compact Disc: 2
Practice Track: 39
Performance Track: 40

HUMOURS OF TULLA

From flutist and former Tulla Ceili Band member Seamus Cooley at Hoban's Tavern November (Chicago 1973).

Compact Disc: 2
Practice Track: 41
Performance Track: 42

THE HUNTER'S HOUSE

A composition by fiddler Ed Reavy, one of the foremost composers of traditional Irish music in the twentieth century, this was heard during a session at the Reavy home in Philadelphia (June 1975) with Ed and son Joe on fiddles.

Jim Kennedy's Favorite

From fiddler Andy O'Brien and Barb (flute) and Bernie (guitar) McDonald during a ceili
at the Focal Point, St. Louis (April 2001); also known as "The Hare's Foot."

Compact Disc: 2
Practice Track: 45
Performance Track: 46

John Stenson's No. 2

*From a session at Jack Quinn's, Newport, Kentucky (October 2000), featuring members of the group Silver Arm—
fiddler Susan Cross, flutist Cindy Matyi, bouzouki player Steve Matyi, and uilleann piper Tim Benson.*

Compact Disc: 2
Practice Track: 47
Performance Track: 48

Johnny Cronin's Fancy

Learned June 1973 from fiddlers Johnny Cronin and Andy McGann, Bunratty Pub, The Bronx, New York

D.C.

Compact Disc: 2
Practice Track: 49
Performance Track: 50

Josie McDermott's Reel

From flutist Larry MacDonagh at Dominic Cosgrove's Public House, Boyle, Roscommon,
this tune commemorates Roscommon flutist Josie McDermott.

Compact Disc: 2
Practice Track: 51
Performance Track: 52

Kitty Gone A-Milking

From a gathering of the Michael Coleman Commemoration along the side of the road between Gurteen and Mullaghroe, Sligo,
featuring more than one hundred musicians from throughout the Irish Musical Diaspora (September 1976).

Compact Disc: 2
Practice Track: 53
Performance Track: 54

LADY ON THE ISLAND

*Heard at St. Patrick's Hall, Columbus, Ohio (May 1993), at a session featuring uilleann piper David Daye
and fiddlers Sandy Jones, Ged Foley, and Ted Jordan.*

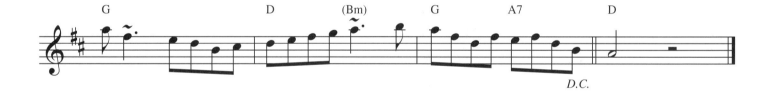

Compact Disc: 2
Practice Track: 55
Performance Track: 56

Last Night's Fun

Heard at the home of flutist Mike McHale, Catskill, New York (October 1994).

D.C.

Compact Disc: 2
Practice Track: 57
Performance Track: 58

Longford Reel

From flutist Patsy Hanley during a session at the Flatley family home, Oak Lawn, Illinois (October 1975).

Compact Disc: 2
Practice Track: 59
Performance Track: 60

LUCY CAMPBELL

From fiddlers Bobby Casey and Andy Boyle, Irish Centre, Camden Town, London, England (March 1972).

Compact Disc: 3
Practice Track: 1
Performance Track: 2

Maid in the Cherry Tree

From pianist Nancy Harling and concertina player Mary Gardiner with dance teachers Mary Ellen Healy and Peggy Roche Boyle in attendance, Chicago (May 1973); also known as "The Curragh Races."

Compact Disc: 3
Practice Track: 3
Performance Track: 4

McFadden's Handsome Daughter

From uilleann piper Kieran O'Hare at a hotel session, Dublin Fest, Dublin, Ohio (August 2000).

D.C.

Compact Disc: 3
Practice Track: 5
Performance Track: 6

The Merry Harriers

From Des O'Connor (tinwhistle), Kit Hodge and Charley Lennon (fiddles),
Bru Na Gael, North St. George's Street, Dublin (May 1972).

Compact Disc: 3
Practice Track: 7
Performance Track: 8

Miss Monaghan

*From fiddler Liz Carroll, uilleann piper Dave Page, and bodhrán player Tommy McMahon
at Dave Page's house, Chicago (May 1973).*

| Compact Disc: 3 |
| Practice Track: 9 |
| Performance Track: 10 |

Miss Thornton

*From accordionist John McGillian and fiddlers John Brennan and Brendan Callahan
at the Plough and the Stars, Philadelphia (November 2000).*

Compact Disc: 3
Practice Track: 11
Performance Track: 12

Molloy's Favorite

From fiddler Kevin Burke at a house party, San Antonio, Texas (June 1983).

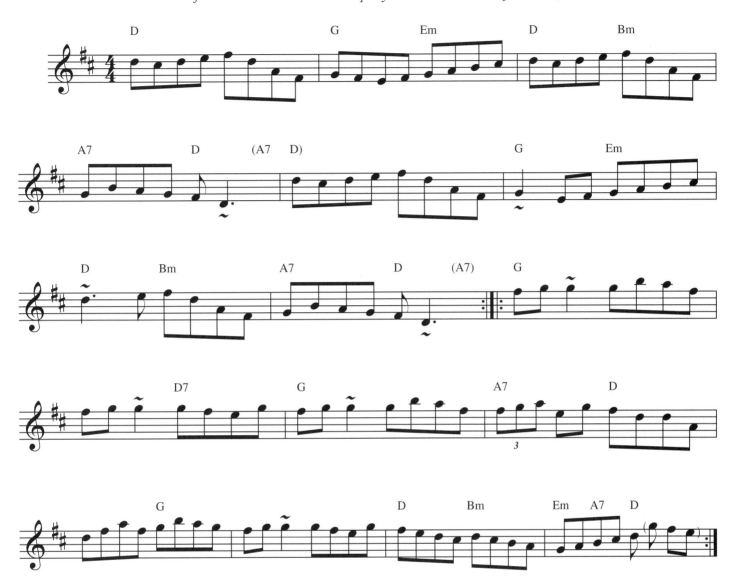

Compact Disc: 3
Practice Track: 13
Performance Track: 14

Money in Both Pockets

From a session at the Neary house, Chicago (September 1975), featuring Jim (fiddle) and Eleanor (piano) Neary
and John McGreevy (fiddle).

Compact Disc: 3
Practice Track: 15
Performance Track: 16

Nine Points of Roguery

Heard at O'Donoghue's Pub, Dublin (October 1971), at a session featuring Mary Bergin (tinwhistle), Paddy O'Brien (accordion), and John Kelly, Sr., and Joe Ryan (fiddles).

| Compact Disc: 3 |
| Practice Track: 17 |
| Performance Track: 18 |

OLD TORN PETTICOAT

From uilleann piper Peter Phelan and fiddler Matt Cranitch during a ceili *at Moran's Hotel, Gardiner Street, Dublin (April 1972).*

Compact Disc: **3**
Practice Track: 19
Performance Track: 20

O'Rourke's Reel

From flutist Dan Foster and fiddler Ralph White, the Omlettry, Austin, Texas (June 1983); also known as "The Wild Irishman."

Compact Disc: 3
Practice Track: 21
Performance Track: 22

OTTER'S HOLT
(Poll an Mhadra Uisce)

A composition of famed Clare fiddler Junior Crehan, heard in the home of husband-and-wife fiddle/step dance duo Kevin and Michelle Crehan, Cincinnati (June 2000), at a session also featuring flutist John Creaven of Galway and the Rolphes Brothers on flute and bodhrán. Along with the melody, there is a verse of poetry that goes:

By my mother's house there was a stream
It's here they'd play music and sit and dream;
From his holt the otter came to listen,
That's why I composed Poll an Mhadra Uisce.

composed by Junior's brother, Vincie, according to Kevin Crehan, Junior's grandson.

THE PRETTY GIRLS OF MAYO

From fiddler Miles Krassen at the wedding of Linda Higginbotham and Bary Kern, Ellettsville, Indiana (February 1974).

Compact Disc: 3
Practice Track: 25
Performance Track: 26

RAKISH PADDY

Heard in December 1977 from fiddler Tony DeMarco at the Eagle Tavern, New York City.

Compact Disc: 3
Practice Track: 27
Performance Track: 28

THE REDHAIRED LASS

From fiddler Dan Collins in August 1978, at McGee's Tavern, New York City.

Compact Disc: 3
Practice Track: 29
Performance Track: 30

Reel of Rio

Heard at a house session with fiddler John Vesey and uilleann piper Thomas Standeven, Philadelphia (1973),
this is a composition of the famed fiddler Sean Ryan of County Laois.

Compact Disc: 3
Practice Track: 31
Performance Track: 32

Sailing into Walpole's Marsh

From harmonica player Eddie Clarke and fiddler Maeve Donnelly at the Festival of American Folklife in Washington, D.C. (July 1976).

| Compact Disc: 3 |
| Practice Track: 33 |
| Performance Track: 34 |

Sheehan's Reel

*Learned from John Fitzpatrick (accordion), Maureen Fitzpatrick (fiddle), and Paddy Kelly (bodhrán)
at the Fitzpatrick home, Massapequa, Long Island, New York (June 1973).*

Compact Disc: 3
Practice Track: 35
Performance Track: 36

THE SILVER SPIRE

From fiddler Andy McGann and pianist Eddie Cruz at the home of Dan Collins, The Bronx (June 1973).

Compact Disc: 3
Practice Track: 37
Performance Track: 38

SPIKE ISLAND LASSIES

From accordionist Billy McComiskey during a session at the Dubliner Hotel, Washington, D.C. (July 1975).

Compact Disc: 3
Practice Track: 39
Performance Track: 40

THE STEAMPACKET

From fiddler John McGreevy and uilleann piper Joe Shannon at the Shannon home on Chicago's Northwestside (July 1975).

Compact Disc: 3
Practice Track: 41
Performance Track: 42

THE SUNNY BANKS

From fiddler Mark Gunther at the First Annual Old-Time Fiddlers Gathering, Battle Ground, Indiana (July 1974).

THE TAILOR'S THIMBLE

From a session at Paddy Reilly's Music Bar, New York City (October 1994), featuring Linda Hickman (flute), Tony DeMarco (fiddle), John Dillon (guitar), and Tom Hanaway (five-string banjo).

Compact Disc: 3
Practice Track: 45
Performance Track: 46

TEAR THE CALICO⊙

From a session at Ireland's 32, Chicago (October 1974), featuring members of the Comhaltas Ceoltoiri Eireann *tour group—accordionist Bobby Gardiner, fiddler Brendan McGlinchey, flutist Peg McGrath, and tinwhistler Deirdre Collis.*

D.C.

Compact Disc: 3
Practice Track: 47
Performance Track: 48

Tim Maloney's Reel

From fiddler Frank Burke at a Hoban's Tavern session, Chicago (April 1975).

Toss the Feathers

From accordionist Jimmy Considine at an Irish Northern Aid concert, Chicago (September 1973).

D.C.

Compact Disc: 3
Practice Track: 51
Performance Track: 52

Touch Me if You Dare

From fiddler Peter Shovlin at an Irish Centre of Pittsburgh session (November 1974).

TRIM THE VELVET

From flutist Seamus Tansey at a hotel dance in Drumkeerin, Leitrim (September 1975).

D.C.

Compact Disc: 3
Practice Track: 55
Performance Track: 56

WEST CLARE REEL

From flute player Paddy Carty in Moylan Brothers Pub, Loughrea, Galway (August 1976).

Compact Disc: 3
Practice Track: 57
Performance Track: 58

WEST CORK REEL

From concertina player Sean O'Dwyer in August 1976 at a pub session in Castletownbere, Cork.

Compact Disc: 3
Practice Track: 59
Performance Track: 60

Within a Mile of Dublin

Learned from uilleann piper Pat Mitchell at a Na Piobairi Uilleann *meeting, Dublin (May1972).*

| Compact Disc: 4 |
| Practice Track: 1 |
| Performance Track: 2 |

An Comhra Donn

From a house session at Chez Cawthorne featuring Armin Barnett (fiddle) and Barry Foy (mandolin),
Chicago (November 1976).

Dunphy's Hornpipe

From flute player Eddie Cahill during a ceili *at the Commodore Barry Club, Irish Centre, Philadelphia (September 1977).*

Compact Disc: 4
Practice Track: 5
Performance Track: 6

The First of May

Heard at a session featuring Frank Claudy (flute), Wendy Morrison (tinwhistle), and Myron Bretholz (bodhrán) at Kelly's Bar, Washington, D.C. (April 1979).

Flowers of Edinburgh

Heard in March 1976 from uilleann piper Al Purcell during a ceili *at the Gaelic League Irish-American Club, Detroit.*

| Compact Disc: 4 |
| Practice Track: 9 |
| Performance Track: 10 |

Greencastle Hornpipe

From piano accordionist Jimmy Keane, Jr., at the Chicago Irish Musicians' Association Picnic, Palos Hills, Illinois (August 1976).

Compact Disc: 4
Practice Track: 11
Performance Track: 12

THE HOME RULER

*Heard from flutist Michael Quinlin, Coach House, Boston (August 1981), this is a composition
of fiddler Frank McCallum of Ballycastle, Antrim.*

Compact Disc: 4
Practice Track: 13
Performance Track: 14

Honeysuckle Hornpipe

Heard at one of the monthly Sunday afternoon sessions hosted by Fr. Charlie Coen in the Rhinecliff Hotel,
adjoining the Amtrak train depot in scenic Rhinecliff, New York (May 1995).

Compact Disc: 4
Practice Track: 15
Performance Track: 16

Humours of Tullycreine

From tenor banjoist Tony Sullivan of Manchester, England, on a visit to Pittsburgh (January 1980).

| Compact Disc: 4 |
| Practice Track: 17 |
| Performance Track: 18 |

Lad O'Beirne's Hornpipe

From fiddlers Andy McGann and Paddy Reynolds at the Philadelphia Ceili Group Irish Music and Dance Festival (September 1976), this is a composition by fiddler Ed Reavy commemorating one of the great Sligo–New York fiddlers of the twentieth century.

Liverpool Hornpipe

*From a session at Corkery's Tavern, Philadelphia, featuring mandolinist/tenor banjoist Mick Moloney
and fiddler Eugene O'Donnell (March 1975).*

| Compact Disc: 4 |
| Practice Track: 21 |
| Performance Track: 22 |

Pretty Maggie Morrissey

From a session at Maggie Mae's, Austin, Texas (October 1986), featuring members of St. James Gate—Fr. Sean Egan (flute),
Jim Fox (concertina), Cliff Moses (hammered dulcimer), Tom McMasters (guitar), and Tom McRae (cittern).

Compact Disc: 4
Practice Track: 23
Performance Track: 24

WHERE DID YOU FIND HER?

From a session at the Irish Traditional Music Festival, North Blenheim, New York (October 1994),
featuring Willie (fiddle) and Siobhan (flute) Kelly.

| Compact Disc: 4 |
| Practice Track: 25 |
| Performance Track: 26 |

John Egan's Polka

Heard at the Golden Ace, Indianapolis, Indiana, featuring uilleann piper Jim Smith and wife Kate on fiddle (February 2000).

Compact Disc: 4
Practice Track: 27
Performance Track: 28

Maggie Pickens

From flutist Elio Matarazzo at the Eighth Step, Albany, New York (June 1995).

Compact Disc: 4
Practice Track: 29
Performance Track: 30

PEG RYAN'S POLKA

From a ceili at Flannery's Bar, New York City (July 1994), featuring Joanie Madden on flute and Fred Rice on fiddle.

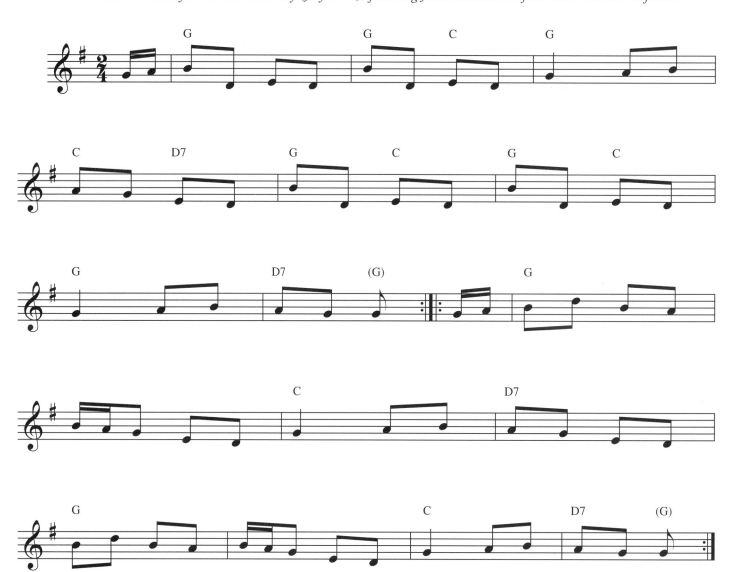

Compact Disc: 4
Practice Track: 31
Performance Track: 32

THE MURROE POLKA

From a session at a Northumbrian Pipers' Gathering, Saugerties, New York (May 1996), featuring Roger Polansky (mandolin),
Helen Stokoe (fiddle), Ernie Shultis (guitar), and Martin Auger (Northumbrian smallpipes).

Compact Disc: 4
Practice Track: 33
Performance Track: 34

Jockey at the Fair

From a session at the North Texas Irish Festival. Dallas, Texas (March 1985), featuring members of Tinker's Dam—Ken Fleming (tenor banjo), Peggy Fleming (fiddle), Earnie Taft (fiddle), and Albert Alfonso (bodhrán).

Madame Bonaparte

Played on tenor banjo by Larry Redican at the Morris family home, Queens, New York (June 1973).

Compact Disc: 4
Performance Track: 37

Caitlin Triall

From Boston harpist Aine Minogue at the Catskills Irish Arts Week, East Durham, New York (July 1995).

THE FLOWER OF MAGHERALLY

From singer Kevin Conneff, Slattery's Pub, Dublin (August 1975).

Compact Disc: 4
Performance Track: 39

Spancil Hill

From singer John McVeay, Dominic Cosgrove's Public House, Boyle, Roscommon (March 1972).

CRESTED HENS
(Bourrée)

Heard in August 1999 at the Irish Rover Pub in Louisville, Kentucky, at a session featuring members of the Rashers,
this beautiful bourrée by French hurdy-gurdy player Gilles Chabenat has been circulating throughout the Irish music world
since its inclusion on the 1996 Solas debut CD.

Compact Disc: 4
Practice Track: 42
Performance Track: 43

Green Grow the Rushes, ☉
(Highland Fling)

Heard from fiddler Tommy Caulfield, Commodore Barry Club, Irish Centre, Philadelphia (September 1977).

Jackets Green
(March)

Learned from flute player Frank Thornton, Chicago, during a visit to the Thornton home (January 1978).

Compact Disc: 4
Practice Track: 45
Performance Track: 46

The Kerry Mills
(Barn Dance)

From a ceili at the Boston Irish Social Club, featuring uilleann piper Owen Frain, accordionists Tom Senier and Jack Martin, fiddlers Pete McKiernan and Jack Carey, with pianist Judy Hogan (June 1973).

Compact Disc: 4
Practice Track: 47
Performance Track: 48

O'Carolan's Draught
(Harp Tune)

From Kathy D'Angelo (harp) and Dennis Gormley (mandolin) during the Philadelphia Ceili Group
Irish Music and Dance Festival (September 1996).

| Compact Disc: 4 |
| Practice Track: 49 |
| Performance Track: 50 |

Slievenamon
(Waltz)

Learned from singer/guitarist Brian Cunningham of the Irish Airs at Dooley O'Toole's, Indianapolis (October 1992).